The Sociology of Wholeness: Emile Durkheim and Carl Jung

David Newcomb

The Sociology of Wholeness:
Emile Durkheim and Carl Jung

LAP LAMBERT Academic Publishing

Impressum/Imprint (nur für Deutschland/ only for Germany)
Bibliografische Information der Deutschen Nationalbibliothek: Die Deutsche Nationalbibliothek
verzeichnet diese Publikation in der Deutschen Nationalbibliografie; detaillierte bibliografische
Daten sind im Internet über http://dnb.d-nb.de abrufbar.
Alle in diesem Buch genannten Marken und Produktnamen unterliegen warenzeichen-, marken-
oder patentrechtlichem Schutz bzw. sind Warenzeichen oder eingetragene Warenzeichen der
jeweiligen Inhaber. Die Wiedergabe von Marken, Produktnamen, Gebrauchsnamen,
Handelsnamen, Warenbezeichnungen u.s.w. in diesem Werk berechtigt auch ohne besondere
Kennzeichnung nicht zu der Annahme, dass solche Namen im Sinne der Warenzeichen- und
Markenschutzgesetzgebung als frei zu betrachten wären und daher von jedermann benutzt
werden dürften.

Coverbild: www.ingimage.com

Verlag: LAP LAMBERT Academic Publishing GmbH & Co. KG
Dudweiler Landstr. 99, 66123 Saarbrücken, Deutschland
Telefon +49 681 3720-310, Telefax +49 681 3720-3109
Email: info@lap-publishing.com

Herstellung in Deutschland:
Schaltungsdienst Lange o.H.G., Berlin
Books on Demand GmbH, Norderstedt
Reha GmbH, Saarbrücken
Amazon Distribution GmbH, Leipzig
ISBN: 978-3-8433-6509-3

Imprint (only for USA, GB)
Bibliographic information published by the Deutsche Nationalbibliothek: The Deutsche
Nationalbibliothek lists this publication in the Deutsche Nationalbibliografie; detailed
bibliographic data are available in the Internet at http://dnb.d-nb.de.
Any brand names and product names mentioned in this book are subject to trademark, brand
or patent protection and are trademarks or registered trademarks of their respective holders.
The use of brand names, product names, common names, trade names, product descriptions
etc. even without a particular marking in this works is in no way to be construed to mean that
such names may be regarded as unrestricted in respect of trademark and brand protection
legislation and could thus be used by anyone.

Cover image: www.ingimage.com

Publisher: LAP LAMBERT Academic Publishing GmbH & Co. KG
Dudweiler Landstr. 99, 66123 Saarbrücken, Germany
Phone +49 681 3720-310, Fax +49 681 3720-3109
Email: info@lap-publishing.com

Printed in the U.S.A.
Printed in the U.K. by (see last page)
ISBN: 978-3-8433-6509-3

The sociology of wholeness: Emile Durkheim and Carl Jung

D. R. Newcomb

To My Sons and Daughters: David, Lori, Cristina, Michael, Nathaniel

.

ACKNOWLEDGEMENTS

I thank Dr. McIntosh, especially for his continuous encouragement and for his example.

I thank Dr. Mestrovic, especially for his unswerving support. In regard to Dr. Mestrovic, I have sought to follow Durhkeim's advice to disciple: "If you wish to mature your thought, attach yourself to the scrupulous study of great master; inquire into a system until you reach its most secret workings."

TABLE OF CONTENTS

2

CHAPTER I

INTRODUCTION

On the following pages, I engage in a sociological discourse of "wholeness" or "integration." The integration or the wholeness of the individual as well as society appears to have been of great interest to Emile Durkheim and to Carl Gustav Jung. On the basis of specific intellectual affinities that will be established between Durkheim and Jung, I will argue that wholeness is a state in which the individual reaches a "balance" of four conceptual levels (balance meaning that each level is acknowledged and integrated into whole person). These four levels are personal consciousness, collective consciousness; the personal unconscious and the collective unconscious (see Fig. 1, next page). It is striking that each of these levels is experienced privately by the individual and yet retains collective qualities to the extent that what are thought of as merely personal-subjective experiences are, in fact, also collective experiences.

THE SPIRIT OF FIN DE SIECLE

The French phrase "fin de siecle" means the end of the century, yet implies the end of an era or the end of a millennium. Special emphasis is placed on the interim period, often conceived of as a decade or so before and after the actual century change. This interim period is symbolic or representative of the ending of one era and beginning another, not just in terms of how physical time is measured (orbits of the sun), but a paralleled ending and a beginning in society of dominant paradigms. The phrase "spirit of fin de siecle" has the connotation of challenge to the existing intelligentsia (Ellenberger 1970). In the spirit of fin de siecle, during the end of the 1800;s, Emile Durkheim challenged the increasingly prevalent Kantian emphasis in science on the "mind" of man/woman at the expense of or the exclusion of the Schopenhauerian concern with the "heart" of man/woman (for detailed discussion see Mestrovic 1992). It seems noteworthy that as Western cultures increasingly changed from agrarian social orders to industrial social orders (especially from the end of the 19th century through the beginning of the 20th century); their scientific communities increasingly concerned themselves with rationality (Weber, [1904] 1958). Durkheim ([1912] 1965) asserted that for science to concern itself only with the rational is, in effect, irrational. For Durkheim, the rational is at best only part of the whole, which includes the irrational and the unconscious (see Mestrovic 1989, 1990).

3

Emile Durkheim's focus and position on the issue of "the mind versus the heart" does not imply that only the "heart" should be considered. Rather, Durkheim takes the holistic position that is not a question of "mind versus heart", but an issue of both "mind and heart". Until recently, this dynamic position has been obscured by time and oversight. In a series of articles and books, Mestrovic has revealed Durkheim to be both a master of empirical science and a champion of metaphysics. In the Coming Fin de Siecle, Mestrovic (1991) suggests that our present era is a fin de siecle in that not only are we into the last decade of the last century of a millennium, but we have not successfully resolved the issues raised by Durkheim a hundred years ago. We have not understood the issues. In the spirit of the Fin de Siecle, Mestrovic calls for a new understanding of the issues, a contemporary understanding rooted in the century old thoughts of Durkheim and his colleagues, including Jung.

METAPHYSICS AND THE HUMAN CONDITION

Metaphysics as used here is defined simply as that which goes beyond known physics. It is my position that human existence is a collective undertaking that has metaphysical qualities. Durkheim and Mauss (1975: Pp. vii-ix) use the following example to illustrate how humans conceptually impose "order" on the world that otherwise appears to be in a constant state of "chaos." A blind adult individual is suddenly able to see for the first time in his/her life. A flood of sensory data in the form of colors, shapes, and images overwhelms the individual. This blur of information is made to appear orderly by imposing classification schemas on the data. So too, I seek greater clarity by imposing a classification system upon human existence. I suggest that human experience, although generally conceived of only on an individual level, is also social, and can be thought of as having four conceptual levels: an individual consciousness, a group consciousness, an individual unconsciousness and a group unconsciousness.

Further, I suggest that these four levels can be reduced to two continua (individual vs. collective, consciousness vs. unconsciousness). Metaphysics is implied throughout this position.

INDIVIDUAL VERSUS GROUP TONTINUUM

In considering the individual versus group continuum it should be remembered that the very concept of an individual only arises within a group context. Although an individual is readily distinguishable as a physical entity from a collectivity, the thoughts, perceptions, definitions and the experiences of the individual are ever connected to the "group" level. What are generally thought of as personal and individualistic – thoughts, perceptions, definitions, experiences – are in fact rooted in the collective consciousness. The collectivity, on the other hand, is dependent upon the continued union with or sharing of its ideas and values by individuals.

CONSCIOUSNESS VERSUS UNCONSCIOUSNESS CONTINUUM

The consciousness versus unconsciousness continuum is also not without conceptual paradox. Although generally we believe that consciousness can easily be distinguished from unconsciousness, the distinction may mask as much as it reveals. As with the individual versus group continuum, in making such singular classifications, each classification appears exclusive from the other. Just as the individual can not in reality be separated from the collective, and the collective cannot be devoid of individuals, consciousness exists only in relation to unconsciousness. Consciousness has inclusive aspects that make it identifiable or exclusive from unconsciousness, and yet our consciousness arises from unconsciousness and our awareness of the unconscious arises through consciousness. Consciousness and unconsciousness, although artificially separable, in fact are interactive process or states, each dependent on the other.

In sum, this dissertation takes the position that from within a social context, classifications or distinctions can be made between groups and the individual, and between the consciousness and the unconsciousness (Jacobi 1973). Further, it is suggested that the human experience includes a personal and a collective consciousness, as well as a personal and a collective unconsciousness. Durkheim, and Jung are mainly invoked here. This paper offers the above as a workable model for the interpretation of social phenomena.

THE FOUR CONCEPTUAL LEVELS

Individual Consciousness

"Society exists and lives only in and through individuals. If the idea of society were extinguished in individual minds and the beliefs, traditions and aspirations of the group were no longer felt and shared by the individuals, society would die." (Durkheim 1915: 389)

Individual consciousness can be conceived as self awareness. The totality of the individual is viewed as exceeding physical, mental and even social levels (Wilber 1981, 1983). To reduce to "blur" of "reality," individual consciousness is conceptually separated from or distinguished from the collective and both levels of the unconscious (individual and collective). Ultimately, however, the individual consciousness remains intricately meshed, web-like with the group or collective conscious level. Nor is individual consciousness actually separable from the individual unconsciousness or the collective unconsciousness due to such interdependence.

Individual consciousness involves self-awareness or a conscious differentiation of self from the collective consciousness. Yet in this process, the individual's consciousness depends directly upon the collective consciousness (conscious collective values, norms, language, concepts, and world view); the individual unconscious (repository of the memories of all personal experiences, repressions, drives, instincts, and links with the collective unconscious); and the collective unconscious (unconscious collective values, norms, repository of collective experiences). Durkheim's disciple, Maurice Halbwachs, implies but does not fully explicate these conceptual distinctions in his Collective Memory (1980).

Definitions of the origins of self-awareness (individual consciousness) vary and depend upon the focus of concern. For example, a geneticist may correctly view the origins of self awareness as having a "chemical trail" that can be traced back to the DNA of our remotest ancestors. However, for the purposes of this discussion, self-awareness or individual consciousness is an interrelated, interacting, and at times, concomitant concept of the proposed model.

I hold the view that there is an emergent quality to self-awareness. Indeed, self-awareness or individual consciousness emerges from a collective context as well as from the unconscious. This is the gist of combining the insights of Durkheim and Jung.

In attempting to define individual consciousness in terms of self-awareness, aspects of the following theorists are considered: Durkheim – Individualism; Mead – the "self". George H. Mead's contributions toward the establishment of American social psychology are widely known. Less known is the logical extension of some of Durkheim's core concepts that Mead's work may represent. Several articles discuss this intellectual connection between Durkheim and Mead (Stone & Farberman 1967, Byne 1976, Mestrovic 1991).

Collective Consciousness

"We speak a language that we did not make; we use instruments that we did not invent; we invoke rights that we did not found; a treasury of knowledge is transmitted to each generation that it did not gather itself, etc. It is to society that we owe these varied benefits of civilization, and if we do not ordinarily see the source from which we get them, we at least know that they are not our own work." (Durkheim 1915, Pp. 242-243)

6

Collective consciousness can be defined as a group or collective awareness. In part, collective consciousness implies an awareness and participation in a collective activity. Usually conceived of as existing on a societal level, other interactive levels of collective consciousness may exist that include a regional level, a state level, a city/county level, a neighborhood level, a family level (Taub-Bynum 1984), even a dyad level to a collectivity.

Many have argued that there already exists a global consciousness as reflected by the potential of the United Nations organization, multi-national corporations, communication networks linking the world into a village of sorts, one language (English) being used as "the" international business language, global environmental concerns, and global concerns for human rights (Featherstone 1988, McLuhan 1989, Harman 1988). However, Durkheim seems also to have been aware of an emergent global collective consciousness:

> "There is no people and no state which is not a part of another society, more or less unlimited, which embraces all the people and all the States with which the
> first comes in contact, either directly or indirectly, there is no national life which is not dominated by a collective life of an international nature." (Durkheim 1915, 475)

As stated earlier, each of the four levels exists in relationship to each other. Although the collective consciousness can be distinguished from the individual level and from the unconscious level, an inseparability of the four components is always implied. The collective consciousness depends on the individual consciousness (the basic element of collective consciousness is individual awareness); the individual unconsciousness (includes the memories of experiences needs that have been met and not met with and by the collective consciousness); the collective unconsciousness (includes those aspects of a society, which the society denies; unconscious collective values & beliefs; and a collective memory).

Individual Unconsciousness

> "We call the unconscious 'nothing,' and yet it is a reality in potential. The thought we shall think, the deed we shall do, even the fate we shall lament tomorrow, all lie unconscious in our today. The unknown in us which the affect uncovers was always there and sooner or later would have presented itself to consciousness. Hence we must always reckon with the presence of things not yet discovered." (Jung [1959] vol. 9, part 1, 1990: 279)

If individual consciousness implies individual awareness, then the individual unconsciousness implies an unawareness on the individual or personal level. However, this personal unconsciousness is more than just a "storage bin" containing the memories of experiences, forgotten and remembered (Wilmer 1987). Just as the individual consciousness is dependent on the collective consciousness, and the collective consciousness is dependent on individual awareness, a similar relationship may exist between the individual unconsciousness and the collective unconsciousness. That is to say, the personal unconsciousness may exist only in the context of a collective unconsciousness. Beyond containing repressed memories of emotionally charged experiences, the individual unconscious remembers all personal experiences as well as its relationship to the collective unconscious. At all times the individual unconscious is interactive with the individual consciousness (which emerges from the individual unconscious), the collective consciousness (collective values, and roles), and the collective unconsciousness (unconscious collective values, and roles).

Collective Unconscious

"The collective unconscious is a part of the psyche which can be negatively distinguished from a personal unconscious by the fact that it does not, like the latter, owe its existence to personal experience and consequently is not a personal acquisition. (Jung [1959] vol.9, 1990: 87)"

The collective unconscious contains aspects that are universal and general. That is, aspects that are found throughout various societies, past and present. The collective unconscious remains meshed with: the individual consciousness (impacting individual conscious behavior), the collective consciousness (denied collective values), and the individual unconscious. Just as the phenomena of individual consciousness occurs only within a collective consciousness, the individual unconscious is interactive with the collective unconscious).

AFFINITIES AMONG DURKHEIM – FREUD – JUNG

This section is intended to sensitize the reader to the fact that Durkheim took part in the intellectual exchange about the unconscious that led to Jung's theoretical formulations. These contributions will be discussed in a later section. Jung and Freud were certainly not the only individuals that were in the forefront of understanding the unconscious around the previous turn-of-the-century, nor was the concept of the unconscious the exclusive domain of psychology (see Ellenberger 1970, Greenwood 1990). The fact that Emile Durkheim advocated the need for sociologists to study the unconscious has been overlooked, ignored, misunderstood, perhaps even suppressed until Stjepan Mestrovic's article on this subject in 1984. With this article and other writings, Mestrovic (1991, 1992) presents a Durkheim that, like Freud and Jung, bridges the last century with the present and the present century with the future. This image of Emile Durkheim is dynamic, daring, contemporary and relevant. As a result of this new image, when speaking of Durkheim's thoughts, phrases like "Durkheim thinks…" or "Durkheim is…" are more appropriate than phrases such as "Durkheim thought…" or "Durkheim was…", for **Durkheim lives!**

Although Durkheim, Freud, and Jung probably never sat in the same room and discussed social concerns, there was an intellectual discourse among them. Durkheim's, Freud's and Jung's interests and concerns with culture or society were always multi-dimensional in scope. Just as Freud and Jung were greatly impacted by Plato's dualisms, so too was Durkheim. Likewise there was a strong Schopenhauerian influence on Durkheim (Magee 1983, Mestrovic 1988, Ellenberger 1970).

Mestrovic (1982, 1988) gives a convincing presentation of the relevance and link between Freud and Durkheim. Both Durkheim and Freud believed in an inner tension within humans, caused by dualities that range from right to wrong and individual concerns versus collective concerns, which are increasing in modern society. Moreover, this inner tension cannot be resolved. Durkheim surpasses even Freud in his pessimism, as indicated by Durkheim's statement:

> "Since the role of the social being in our single selves will grow ever more important as history moves ahead, it is wholly improbable that there will ever be an era in which man is required to resist himself to a lesser degree, an era in which he can live a life that is easier and less full of tension. To the contrary, all evidence compels us to expect our effort in the struggle between the two beings within us to increase with the growth of civilization." (Durkheim 1914, in Bellah 1973: 163)

Jung however, believed that this inner tension, though increasing, could be resolved through the fusion of dualities. Durkheim's position implicitly allows for the possibility of such a fusion of opposites, but explicitly doubts that it will happen. Durkheim, Freud, and Jung individually considered themselves to be students of culture and addressed sociological concerns. Durkheim and Freud paralleled each other in their work on religion. Not only did Freud read Durkheim, he also cited Durkheim a number of times in his Totem and Taboo.

Similar constructs and interpretations of "reality" link Durkheim and Jung in such a way that one is complemented by the other (Greenwood 1990, Progoff 1953, Staude 1976, Gaula 1970). A major concern with the unconscious is a common theme for both Durkheim and Jung, not to mention Freud. The development of one of Jung's most important concepts, archetypes, can be linked to Durkheim's concept of collective representations – and to Lucien Levy-Bruhl (Mestrovic 1985: p. 206, 1988: p. 99)

(CW, vol. 91, p. 5). Levy-Bruhl was a mutual friend of Jung's and Durkheim's and may have provided a foundation for both men's theories. According to Mestrovic (1988), Durkheim ([1938] 1977) liked using Jung's term collective unconscious and Jung liked using Durkheim's term collective unconsciousness. Mestrovic (1988: p. 96) states "for Durkheim science lies on the continuum of conscious-unconscious. It is the process of wrenching knowledge from the unknown and the unconscious." Not only is this statement congruent with Jung's thoughts, but Jung might add that the same is true for meaningful human existence. Meaningful existence or wholeness for Jung, though never free from pain and suffering, is made possible by bringing into consciousness that which is unconscious.

All three individuals were products of 19th century Western European bourgeoisie culture. Yet each, in significant ways, transcended their own time period to bridge the gap with the 20th century. Although only Freud and Jung were trained medical doctors, Durkheim never tired of using medical metaphors with skill and precision. Each of the three was steeped in the classics, especially Plato. Plato's thoughts on dualisms greatly influenced Durkheim, Freud (Mestrovic 1982) and Jung. Schopenhauer's concentration on duality provides another link among Durkheim, Freud and Jung.

Almost a hundred years have past since Durkheim presented his concepts of collective representations and the collective consciousness. Freud's concept of the unconscious was introduced also and it has been almost as long since Jung introduced his concepts of the archetype and the collective unconscious. Although contemporary societies are on the threshold of the twenty-first century, we appear far from fully understanding and applying such concepts.

DISPOSITIONAL TERMS

Terms or concepts used by Durkheim, Freud and Jung (such as consciousness, the unconscious, collective consciousness, collective unconscious, collective representations and archetypes) are dispositional terms. To attempt clarification of present and future confusion, such terms are never "genus proximum and differentia specifica" (Willer 1968: p. 178). As Willer (1968) has pointed out, a dispositional term derives its meaning from empirical indicators and how it is used in conjunction with other theoretical concepts. Therefore, the meaning of a dispositional term can never be final or exact because of unending connections with other theoretical terms. A dispositional term is not an empirical category, but is a theoretical concept that is indicated by certain empirical phenomena.

"It is not the universal presence of phenomena which is crucial to Durkheim but the universal connection of indicators to their concepts which is seen as essential for their definition." (Willer 1968: p. 180)

Further, Willer adds that only recently have dispositional terms come to be recognized in the social sciences. Singling out Durkheim, Willer praises his genius for the correct use of dispositional terms decades before their general recognition. Freud and Jung similarly demonstrated their genius as well.

In the next section, Chapter II, the individual or personal consciousness will be considered in depth.

CHAPTER II

INDIVIDUAL CONSCIOUSNESS

"All internal life draws its primary material from without. All we can think of is objects or our conceptions of them. We cannot reflect our own consciousness in a purely undetermined state... Now consciousness becomes determined only when affected by something not itself. Therefore, if it individualizes beyond a certain point, if it separates itself too radically from other beings, men or things, it finds itself unable to communicate with the very source of its normal nourishment... It creates nothingness within by creating it without." ([1915] 1966, p. 279)

PROBLEMS IN DEFINING THE TERM INDIVIDUAL CONSCIOUSNESS

The concept of individual consciousness is an artificial separation from the "whole" (i.e. the individual unconscious; the collective conscious; and the collective unconscious), and yet the concept of individual consciousness, although only a "part," has its own Sui generic properties. Still, the whole (comprised of the four mentioned concepts) represents a Sui generic whole that appears not to be diminished when its very aspects are viewed as "being more than the sum of their parts." In generalizing from Durkheim's statement that science is wrenching into consciousness that which is unconscious, I hold that all of us experience consciousness by wrenching it from unconsciousness. To which I add that similarly, what we consider to be our individuality is actually wrenched from the/our collectivity. Further, I suggest that individual consciousness, in no small part, is wrenched from the individual's unconscious as well as their collective consciousness and his/her collective unconscious.

Other problems exist in discussions of individual consciousness, including the idea that individual consciousness ultimately implies awareness beyond self awareness. Also, because the experience of consciousness is experienced individually, there exist a wide range of experiences, all of which—although different—constitute individual consciousness. Therefore, for the purposes of this discussion, the notion of individual consciousness is limited to awareness of "self." Self will be defined in more sociological than psychological terms.

TOWARD A CLARIFICATION OF INDIVIDUAL CONSCIOUSNESS

A number of people have addressed the fragmentation of and the tepid nature of contemporary sociology and a few have even addressed remedies. Durkheim's sociology may be such a remedy. Most

American sociological theory textbooks incorrectly criticize Durkheim for presenting an "over socialized" (Wrong 1961) version of the individual, and even claim that he ignored or neglected the subject of the individual. Yet a close associate of Durkheim's Paul Fauconnet ([1922] 1958, p. 32) suggested that "individualism" might be an appropriate name for Durkheim's sociology. Revealing the influence of Plate and Schopenhauer, Durkheim (1914) portrayed individualism as a duality, homo duplex, that comprises a whole, not one or the other, but both. Durkheim (1924) deals with the individual in general or collectively (sociology) and avoids dealing with a specific individual (psychology). According to Durkheim,

"So we are really made up of two beings facing in different and almost contrary directions, on of whom exercises a real pre-eminence over the other. Such is the profound meaning of the antithesis which all men have more or less clearly conceived between the body and the soul, the material and the spiritual beings who coexist within us." (Durkheim, [1915] 1965, p. 298)

In this quote Durkheim sets the poles of homo duplex as body versus soul which seems akin in some ways to Schopenhauer's duality of mind versus heart, as well as Plato's many dualisms. Compatible with this notion is Durkheim's distinction of "individualism" as composed of the two diametrical opposites, collective representations versus subjective will (Mestrovic 1988).

If Durkheim's notion of individualism is not conceived as dualism or home duplex, misunderstanding and distortion will likely result. For example, consider home duplex in terms of its collective and individual aspects. In "Individualism and Intellectuals", Durkheim ([1898] 1973) introduces the duality of how intellectuals view individualism versus how he thinks individualism should be viewed. Within this home duplex, Durkheim presents another home duplex, which is a homo duplex within a homo duplex. In one regard Durkheim stresses the importance of the collectivity:

"For it is exceedingly clear that all communal life is impossible without the existence of interests superior to those of the individual." (Durkheim [1898] 1973: p. 43)

However, just a few pages later, Durkheim stresses the importance of the individual:

"Each of us incarnates something of humanity, each individual consciousness contains something divine and thus finds itself marked with a character which renders it sacred and inviolable to others." (Durkheim [1898] 1973: p. 52)

Although one statement may appear to be at odds with the other, they actually complement one another in such a way that when considered together, they come closer to capturing the fullness of social "reality" than if considered alone. By looking at Durkheim's position on the importance of the collectivity and not understanding the importance of the individual, it would be quite easy to incorrectly conclude that Durkheim devalues the individual, in spite of what he says. The complementing opposite misinterpretation, (although usually no one has accused Durkheim of this, in part because his position on individualism has not been well understood) would be to accuse Durkheim of doing psychology. It is only by reconciling these opposites then, that for Durkheim a clearer image of the society emerges. Alpert seems to reflect this duality and its synthesis with the words:

"Man he [Durkheim] insisted, is a product as well as a creature of society, and consequently, a theory of human nature must be the end result and not the starting point of a science of sociology." (1958, p. 235)

This same type of duality or home duplex is seen with the seemingly conflictive, yet complementary notions: collective representations versus individual representations (Parker 1989, Pp. 94-105).

Collective Representations

Durkheim's concept of collective representations bears a striking relationship or counterpart to Jung's archetypes and will be discussed in more detail later. Here however, the similarity between Durkheim's collective representation and Mead's notion of symbolic interpretation will be reviewed.

Both Durkheim and Mead are at odds with the most basic of psychological orthodoxy, the "stimulus-response model." That is to say, in the psychological perspective shaped by Pavlov, it is accepted that a stimulus produces human behavior or response. This is much too simplistic a model of human behavior because an "interpretation" of the stimulus is missing as the link between "stimulus-response." For Durkheim and Mead, "stimulus-then-interpretation-response" would be a more correct model of human behavior. Durkheim uses the idea of employing collective representations for the interpretation of "reality," while Mead uses symbols. It may not be an overstatement to say that collective representations are symbols and symbols are collective representations. It is no that the collective representation or symbol reflects as a mirror the stimulus; rather, the collective representation or symbol refracts, like a prism, the stimulus. Likewise, all that is objective is comprehended subjectively through collective representation or symbols. Hence the importance of Durkheim stressing repeatedly that we can never know the "world" except through representations. The thrust of Mead's writing was to develop a social theory of mind and self based within the context of language (Crescimanno 1982). One would be hard pressed to find anything more symbolic or representational than language.

Specifically, it is the "cult of the individual" that for Durkheim is the collective representation that "represents" the positive side of the individualism "coin." The phrase "cult of the individual" may seem today an apt description of the negative aspect individualism (subjective or narcissistic will). However, for Durkheim, the phrase represented the endowment of rights, dignity and increased autonomy upon the general individual by society. As a representation, the cult of the individual is rooted deeply in democratic principles. "Liberty" and "the pursuit of happiness" are correctly assumed in American society to be individual rights. Yet what is often overlooked is that source and guarantor of such individual right is the collectivity. Liberty is but "institutionalized autonomy" and the pursuit of happiness is actually "institutionalized individual initiative" (Logan 1987). For Durkheim, the individual can only become an individual when his/her subjective will or narcissistic will is restrained, and when he or she lives in a society that enshrines individual dignity and rights through collective representations.

Subjective Will

The subjective will commonly represents the essence of the individual. But not so for Durkheim, who viewed the subjective will as primitive, undisciplined, selfish, narcissistic and in need of control. At the extreme, it can be thought of as a mixture of Herbert Spencer's subjectivism (reality only existing subjectively) and the "me generation" ("if it feels good, do it!") movement of late.

To Durkheim, the subjective will, like Freud's "id", is fundamentally rooted in the biology of the individual. However, it is not biology that gives rise to and sustains the egoistic or subjective will; it is society. For Durkheim and Freud, norms can only be effective when they are internalized by individuals. Internalized norms will work only when they are respected, attractive (Durkheim) or erotically charged (Freud). Mere existence of rules does not guarantee social order. The appetites are insatiable and can be controlled by Freud's "ego", or by the individual internalizing the collective norms and values (collective representation – social facts). Society either provides the "high road" of collective representations for the generalized individual or the "low road" of egoism. Durkheim leaves no doubt that individualism is a collective phenomenon that evolves through the division of labor within society:

> "Originally society is everything, the individual nothing ... man is considered only an instrument in its hands ... But gradually things change. As societies become greater in volume and density, they increase in complexity, work is divided, individual differences multiply, and the moment approaches when the only remaining bond among the members of a single human group will be

that they are all men... Our dignity as moral beings is ... no longer the property of the city-state; but it has ... become our property." (Durkheim [1897] 1951, p. 336)

Although the individual may seem to be viewed as separate from the collective, Durkheim states that the individual is ever part of the whole.

"In fact, all are consciousness, which express one and the same object, the world; and the world itself is only a system of representations, each particular consciousness is really only the reflection of the universal consciousness. However, each one expresses it from its own point of view, and in its own manner." (Durkheim [1915] 1965, p. 306)

A review of Logan's article of the historical evolution of the sense of "self" supports Durkheim's assertion that individualism has developed within collective or social context. Historically, according to Logan, concern with the "self" has tended to be limited to either "self-as-object" or "self-as-subject". It was Mead who suggested "self" as a dualistic model consisting of both "self-as-object" (I) or "self-as-subject" (me). "Self" was discovered during the Middle Ages, depending on who you read. Prior to the late Middle Ages, an individual's identity was more of a group identity rather than individual. The first experience of the sense of "self" probably was little more than an awareness of being separate from the corporation or church. During the Age of Reason and the Enlightenment (17th and 18th centuries), the "self" began to take on a few of the qualities that define it as a unique individuality. The "I" was emphasized as being able to initiate and conduct thought and systematically observe the "world". The liberal tradition from Locke to Jefferson and the accompanying "new" idea that the individual can "reason, know, and choose" was instrumental in establishing democracy in America. Not everyone, however, agrees with this assessment. In particular, Alexis de Tocqueville believed that democracy was rooted in particular "habits of the heart" (see Bellah 1985). The "self" was beginning to involve an inner quality, but for the most part this inner self was limited to the "mind" of the individual. For some writers, the late 18th century (the Romantic period), better represents the beginning of the "self" because of a shift from seeing "self" as subject to seeing "self" as object. Rousseau, Goethe and Kant each developed definitions of the "self" that included both subjective and objective aspects. By the 19th century, a "self" was seen as unique but was shaped by the external "world". With the Existentialism and Post Modernism of the 20th century, the "self" has become alienated from "itself". That is the "I" becomes alienated from "me". G. H. Mead's dualistic model of "self" includes both "self-as-object" and "self-as-subject."

Another way of viewing Durkheim's position on how individualism is shaped by society is to concentrate on the collective consciousness.

16

CHAPTER III

COLLECTIVE CONSCIOUSNESS

"The personality can be itself only to the degree in which it is a social entity that is autonomous in action. It is true that in one sense it receives everything from without – its moral and its material energies. Just as we can sustain our physical life only by the aid of sustenance taken from the cosmic milieu, so do we give sustenance to our mental life only by the aid of ideas and sentiments that reach us from the social milieu. Nothing yields nothing, and the individual left to his own devices could not raise himself beyond his own level." (Durkheim [1950] 1983, p. 90)

Durkheim's term for collective consciousness, "conscience collective", can best be grasped if viewed as a dispositional term (Willer 1968). Otherwise the varying, partial definitions offered by many theorists can only continue to obscure as much or more than what they have revealed. Over fifty years ago, Alpert (1939) stated that Durkheim was well known among American sociologists but that Durkheim was not known well. This statement still has some applicability today, particularly with the concept of collective consciousness and the related concept of collective representations.

Confusion begins when the French term "conscience collective" is first approached, due to the definition of the French word "conscience" and "consciousness." Therefore, when aspects of the collective consciousness, such as the collective representations – collective beliefs and collective sentiments – are considered, two distinct meanings are implied. Conscience refers to a moral or religious significance, while consciousness refers to cognition (Lukes, 1972, p. 318). The collective consciousness then consists of collective representations that encompass both aspects "mind" (beliefs) and "heart" (sentiments).

According to LaCapra (1972), Durkheim applies the term collective consciousness only to "normal" or "healthy" societies, not "pathological" or "sick" societies. It is alleged that Durkheim views the normal society as one in which its collective representations – including symbols, values, norms – maintain a tense balance within the collective consciousness (LaCapra, 1972, p. 241). By implication, a sick or pathological society would lack a collective consciousness. In contrast to LaCapra, Mestrovic (1988) maintains that an anomic society is a sick or deranged society for Durkheim, such that its collective consciousness is also abnormal. Durkheim's position is analogous, in some ways, to Erich Fromm's (1955) claim that entire societies may be considered sick (although Fromm draws on Marx and Freud, not Durkheim).

Durkheim, Freud, and Jung offer very compatible statements on the nature of a collective consciousness:

"The totality of beliefs and sentiments common to average citizens of the same society forms a determinate system which has its own life; one may call it the collective or common conscience ... It is, independent of the particular conditions in which individuals are placed; they pass on and it remains ... it connects successive generations with one another. It is, thus an entirely different thing from particular consciences, although it can be realized only through them." (Durkheim [1893] 1964, p. 79-80)

"Whoever be the individuals that compose it, however like or unlike ... the fact that they have been transformed into a group puts them in possession of a sort of collective mind which makes them feel, think and act in a manner quite different from that in which each individual ... would feel, think and act were he in ... isolation." (Freud 1964, p. 73)

"Just as the individual is not merely a unique and separate being, but is also a social being, so the individual phenomenon, but a collective one ... the universal similarity of human brains leads to the universal possibility of a uniform mental functioning. This functioning is the collective mind and the collective soul. (By the collective mind, I mean collective thinking ...; by the collective soul, I mean collective feeling ...; and by the collective psyche, I mean the collective psychological functions as a whole.)" (Jung, CW, vol. 7, p. 275)

Durkheim, Freud and Jung appear to be in agreement that the collective consciousness (collective mind for Freud or collective psyche for Jung) is a collective phenomena that is made manifest through individuals. These three theorists also elevate to the collective level what may be thought of as the most individualistic of phenomenon ("thinking" and "feeling" or "beliefs" and "sentiments").

COLLECTIVE CONSCIOUSNESS AND COLLECTIVE REPRESENTATIONS

"The society that we have made into the object of moral conduct goes incalculably beyond the level of individual interests. What we should above all cherish in it is not its body but its mind. And what is called the mind of a society is nothing other than a collection of ideas which the individual in isolation would never have been able to conceive and which outstrip the limits of his mentality, and are shaped and given life only by the coming together of a great number of associated individuals." (Durkheim [1925] 1963, p. 140)

It is necessary to recognize that Durkheim never offered a definitive explanation for collective consciousness. Nor could he, since collective consciousness is an ever expanding dispositional term

(Willer 1968). Durkheim was a 19th century pioneer and explorer, so advanced in his thinking that we in the late 20th century are only beginning to catch up to him. At the time Einstein was expanding the

frontiers of physics, Freud was expanding the frontiers of understanding human societies. Durkheim's concepts of collective consciousness and collective representations are on par in importance with Freud's concept of consciousness and the unconscious, and Einstein's new understanding of physics. Whereas Freud begins with a theory of human nature, Durkheim begins with the level of structure or society and ends with a theory of human nature (Alpert 1958).

Judith Willer has pointed out that Durkheim never defined "collective consciousness" in "genus proximum and differentia specifica" terms and that it simply is not possible to do so with all scientific terms. Her position is that not only is there a problem because of an ever expanding definition of collective consciousness, but that critics of Durkheim have overlooked the possibility that terms such as collective consciousness are subject to further development. Willer states (1968, p. 289):

> "We cannot understand his [Durkheim's] work by simply comparing him with his contemporaries – he pioneered a path of his own, the intricacies of which are still being analyzed ... He cannot be understood in terms of the sociology of today – its 'assumptions' block off entrance to a new level of understanding."

Mestrovic, in discussing the content of the collective consciousness, collective representations, echoes a similar view of Durkheim's thinking with the statement:

> "He [Durkheim] was truly ahead of his time. Collective representations have not had a chance to catch up with him, because the representations he was using in his teachings were hardly born in his lifetime." (Mestrovic, 1988, p. 26)

Durkheim's actual notion of collective representations is also quite different from what is presented in secondary texts. Representations for Durkheim are the "phenomena that bridge the individual-society distinction in the form of social facts" (Mestrovic: 1982, p. 4). That is to say that social facts are collective representations. However, interpreters have tended to use the term social facts instead of collective representations to denote purely objective and social phenomena.

Durkheim's basic position on representations can be summed as follows:

"1. Representations exist as an order of natural phenomena following their own laws;

2. Their existence implies a relationship with their substrata, but not a dependence upon it;

3. Representations are caused and in turn are causes;

4. The mind, being one such representation, is not to be reduced to its substrata;

5. Since representations exist Sui generic, the mind must somehow store past representations, [Durkheim] hints at the concept of the unconscious" (Mestrovic, 1982, p. 105).
It is important to not that the notion of consciousness is not inherent in the idea of a representation (Mestrovic 1984, p. 267-7). In fact collective representations are unknown to the consciousness:

"We can never know objects in the world as things-in-themselves, but as representation ... Durkheim ... regarded representations as phenomena (Mestrovic 1985, p. 206).
For Durkheim, the collective consciousness is itself a collective representation.

CHAPTER IV

THE INDIVIDUAL UNCONSCIOUS

"Within everyone one of us, then, there is at all times a host of ideas, tendencies and habits that act upon us without our knowing exactly how or wherefore. To us they are hardly perceptible and we are unable to make out their differences properly. They lie in the subconscious. They do however affect our conduct and there are even individuals who are moved solely by these motives." (Durkheim [1950] 1983, p. 80)

In considering such a concept as the "individual unconscious," it seems that the advertising men/women of Madison Avenue are considerably more adept at understanding and employing principles involving this subject than the social scientist. Few, if any, on Madison Avenue know of Durkheim or that he wrote of the insatiable human appetite for "things," how acquiring stimulates rather than satisfies human desires. Yet it is doubtful that there are any people working on Madison Avenue who don't understand this basic fact. No doubt, Freud is scoffed at on Madison Avenue as he is in most of America for his emphasis on the unconscious human concern with sexuality and aggression. Although "family values" have been highly exploited over the last decade or so, sex and aggression remain the staple collective representations manipulated by Madison Avenue. Nor are Jung and his notions of the individual/collective unconscious and of archetypes probably well known on Madison Avenue. But where and who applies or appeals to these basic ideas to a larger extent than Madison Avenue? I hasten to state that my intention here is not to participate in Madison Avenue "bashing," but to point out that unconscious principles stated by Durkheim, Freud and Jung – while debated still in academia – are being successfully applied to others. Perhaps the term "misapplied" would be more appropriate, considering that Durkheim, Freud and Jung sought to liberate the human spirit rather than continue or increase its enslavement.

It is with some irony that any discussion of the unconscious seems to render it part of consciousness. So that to consciously discuss the unconscious may mean that what was part of the unconscious is now part of consciousness. However this was precisely Freud's and Jung's active goal.

Depending upon one's perspective, Freud deserves the credit or the blame for "popularizing" the concept of the individual unconscious. However, as a concept, the subject of the unconscious was not new when Freud refined it (Ellenberger 1970). Freud reached a point in his professional life when he felt that there was much in human existence that consciousness could not account for. In this hidden, inaccessible, unconscious area, location unknown are the repressed fears, feelings, motives, and desires that made themselves known indirectly through slips-of-the-tongue, jokes, dreams, and fantasies. Through a technique that Freud called "free association"; a patient would say what ever came to mind, regardless of the context or subject matter. From the random, seemingly unconnected statements patters emerged that provided a glimpse into the patient's unconscious. After developing a simple model of the human mind consisting of consciousness-unconsciousness, Freud developed his more sophisticated and now famous id-ego-super ego model (Freud [1923] 1974). Although the ego and super ego are not truly separate from the unconscious, it is the id that is mostly what Freud originally defined as the unconscious. However in the three-fold model, the word "unconscious" is no longer used as a known but as an adjective. For Freud, the original notion of the id may have been derived from Schopenhauer's concept of the will (Mestrovic, 1991) and the term id may have come from Nietzsche (Ellenberger, 1970 p. 277) but, Freud claims to have borrowed the concept id from George Groddeck (Ellenberger 1970, p. 516).

Freud first considered the unconscious to be a repository of repressed memories, drives, and tendencies. In developing the concept of the id, Freud added unconscious feelings and fantasies (Ellenberger, 1970, p. 516). Freud and Jung may be in agreement on the point that the unconscious is more significant than consciousness in reference to the human mind. However, the way the unconscious is viewed by Jung is different from Freud's view.

Jung's model of personality also has been presented as a three fold model (Levin 1978), consisting of the ego, the personal unconscious, and the collective unconscious. The conscious mind is represented by the ego, which contains personal experiences, thoughts, and feelings. The unconscious is viewed not only as personal but collective. For Jung, as for Freud, the personal unconscious contains all of the repressed personal material for Jung. A main point of divergence between Freud and Jung is the notion of a collective unconscious, which is not private and personal but is held in common by our species. Although Freud did not use the term "collective unconscious" explicitly, he sometimes implied it, as in Totem and Taboo, wherein he had to explain how ancient psychic traits survived through the centuries.

Few scholars have understood and even fewer have written concerning Durkheim's use of concepts unconscious and collective representations and how they relate to Jungian concepts. However, Mestrovic (1982, 1984, 1985, 1988) has laid the foundation for such an understanding, and in fact

Mestrovic calls for a "reformation of sociology" based on this understanding. Also Greenwood (1990) has skillfully applied Durkheim's and Jung's complementary notions to a specific area of the sociology of

religion. In the remaining pages of this section, Durkheim's concern with the unconscious and collective representations will be reviewed.

DURKHEIM: THE UNCONSCIOUS & COLLECTIVE REPRESENTATION

"When collective ideas and sentiments are obscure or unconscious, when they are scattered piecemeal throughout the society, they resist change. They elude any action because they elude consciousness: they cannot be grasped because they are in the shadows." (Durkheim [1950] 1983, p. 87)

From Parsons to Lukes, according to Mestrovic, at best only a partial Durkheim has been presented, at worst a total distortion of Durkheim has been presented in secondary texts. Interpreters of Durkheim have overlooked or missed the fact that for Durkheim, the concept of the unconscious is unequivocally necessary to sociology. Mestrovic lays out the four steps to Durkheim's "radical methodology". The four steps are:

1. Durkheim begins by challenging the popular, subjective opinions and those of scholars concerning the topic(s).
2. Durkheim next sets up the problem so that the accounts of witnesses, agents, even society's opinion are not important. In this way, he develops 'an angle' on the problem.
3. Durkheim next takes a social fact, defined to exclude subjective factors, and explains it (showing "what causes it, what its function is, from what ideas and sentiments it is derived and what needs it meets" Durkheim [1907] 1980, p. 140).
4. Finally, Durkheim offers what he considers a scientific re-formulation of the problem so that constructive social change may occur. (Mestrovic 1984, pp. 277-278)

Durkheim emphasizes that "the theme of the unconscious enters into every step of the sequence" (Mestrovic, 1984, p. 277). For Durkheim, the unconscious totally engulfs the conscious (Mestrovic 1984, p. 279). Mestrovic states than an understanding of Durkheim's use of the unconscious will do two things for sociology: first, a parsimony in understanding Durkheim may be achieved and second, it can also add sophistication to Durkheim's sociological theories (Mestrovic 1984, p. 282).

The following quotes from Durkheim about representations could have been written by Jung about archetypes.

"The representation, it is maintained, has no power of retaining itself as such. When a sensation, image, or idea is no longer presented to us it ceases to exist, without leaving the slightest trace. The organic impression which preceded the representation does not, however, disappear completely. What remains is a modification of the nerve elements involved which will predispose them to vibrate again as they vibrated on the first occasion" (Durkheim [1924] 1974, p. 4).

Here Durkheim, as Jung with regard to archetypes, suggests that representations exist on an organic or biological level before they exist as a "sensation, image, or idea". Further, he suggests that once representations are consciously experienced, biological changes take place in "nerve elements" that make the individual receptive to future exposure.

"Our direction is guided not by the few ideas that hold our attention, but by the residues of our past: the habits which we have contracted, the prejudices, the tendencies which motivate us and for which we cannot completely account to ourselves" (Durkheim [1924] 1974, p. 6)

Again like Jung and his notion of archetypes, Durkheim claims that human beings cannot be separated from those generations that have gone before. Through representations, continuity over time and throughout society is maintained.

"If [representations] have the power to react directly upon each other and to combine according to their own laws, they are then realities which, while maintaining an intimate relation with their substratum, are to a certain extent independent of it." (Durkheim [1924] 1974, p. 23)

Here Durkheim points to the complexity and dynamic quality of representations (archetypes for Jung). I believe that embodied in this statement is one of Jung's main points about archetypes. Also, this is one of Jung's more difficult points to understand, namely that the contents of archetypes or representations can and do change, but the form remains the same. For example, the concept of "the family" can be viewed as an archetype or as a collective representation. When compared globally or over time, the contents of what a "family" is varies greatly, yet the form of what a "family" is remains recognizable.

CHAPTER V

THE COLLECTIVE UNCONSCIOUS

Obscure sentiments which are diffusive by nature, the many habits acquired, resist any change precisely because they are obscure. What cannot be seen is not easily modified. All these states of mind shift, steal away, cannot be grasped, precisely because they are in the shadows. On the other hand, the more the light penetrates the depths of social life, the more can changes be introduced." (Durkheim [1950] 1983, p. 84)

This section will begin with an overview of Jung's theories of the collective unconscious and archetypes. It will be followed by a more in depth examination of these two concepts and what makes them sociologically relevant. Many authors who have written about Jung and his work note the difficulty in defining or discussing such abstract concepts as the collective unconscious and archetypes. One problem is that by definition these concepts transcend human consciousness. Also, in such discussions we must use language to convey our thoughts, and language is at best a symbolic representation that can only "mirror" that which we attempt to define. By "mirror" I am suggesting that as a mirror can only reflect a two dimensional image of our three dimensional "world", so too are "words" unable to reflect the full depth of concepts.

Just as the concept collective consciousness infers the concept of collective representations, the use of the concept collective unconscious infers the use of the concept archetypes. Likewise the use of the concept archetype infers the use of the concept collective unconscious. As language(s) consist of words, so too the collective unconscious consists of symbols known as archetypes and the collective consciousness consists of collective representations. Also, just as language itself involves words, the collective unconscious involves archetypes, and the collective consciousness involves collective representation. According to Jung:

"For Freud ... the unconscious is of an exclusively personal nature ... A more or less superficial layer of the unconscious is undoubtedly personal. I call it the personal unconscious. But this personal unconscious rests upon a deeper layer, which does not derive from personal experience and is not a personal acquisition but is inborn. This deeper layer I call the collective unconscious. I have chosen the term 'collective' because this part of the unconscious is not individual but universal; in contrast to the personal psyche, it has contents and modes of behavior that are more or less the same everywhere and in all individuals. It is, in other words, identical in all men (humans) and thus constitutes a common psychic substrate of a suprapersonal nature which is present in every one of us." (CW, vol 9 I, par. 3)

To paraphrase Jung, Freud's contribution to the understanding of the unconscious was limited to the individual or personal unconscious. What Freud thought to be the total unconscious was in fact only one dimension. Deeper into the unconscious lies the collective dimension. This collective unconscious is shared by everyone at all times. We collectively acquire the collective unconscious through biological "wiring."

Jung's theory of the collective unconscious was based on his empirical observations and experiences. Analysis of patients' hallucinations and analysis of dreams were the basis for his theory (Goldbrunner 1966, p. 77). Likewise, this same evidence contributed to his theory of archetypes, for the collective unconscious does not exist without archetypes and archetypes do not exist without the collective unconscious. A specific hallucination and a specific dream will now be discussed in an attempt to introduce the concept of archetype and to tie it to the concept of collective unconscious.

THE COLLECTIVE UNCONSCIOUS & ARCHETYPES

Around 1906 Jung treated a paranoid schizophrenic patient whose background was well-known. One day the patient, while looking out a window, asked Jung to come and look out the window. Jung looked and saw nothing unusual. The patient was surprised and said "Surely you see the sun's penis – when I move my head to and fro, it moves too, and that is where the wind comes from". Jung thought this is a strange notion and made a note of it. Then in 1910, while pursuing mythological studies, Jung read a recently published book that contained a translated ancient Greek papyrus text dealing with religious ritual. The text read:

> "The path of the visible gods will appear through the disc of the sun, who is God my father. Likewise the so-called tube, the origin of the ministering wind. For you will see hanging down from the disc of the sun something that looks like a tube. And towards the regions westward it is as though there were an infinite east wind. But if the other wind should prevail towards the regions of the east, you will in like manner see the vision veering in that direction." (CW, vol. 9 I, p. 51)

It was considered impossible for the patient to have had prior knowledge of the Greek text; hence, Jung believed that he had discovered something significant. Indeed, as his knowledge of reoccurring myths increased, he continued to find parallels with patients' hallucinations. This suggested that at times hallucinating patients somehow ere tapping into an unconscious level that appeared to involve a collective history. The contents of this type of hallucination Jung called archetypal – implying a consistency of form. That is to suggest that the form of the archetypal image remains the same through time and space (cultures) although the contents may change. For example, the image hanging from the sun was seen by the ancient Greeks as a tube, and Jung's patient interpreted the image as a penis.

In the analysis of patients' dreams, Jung constantly encountered dreams and contents of dreams that could not be explained on a personal level. However when considered in terms of a collective unconscious level, the meaning of these dreams seemed quite clear (Bennet 1967). While in the unconscious state of sleeping, then, both personal and collective images, symbols, or archetypes are available to the dreamer. For Jung, dreams are empirical evidence of the existence of archetypes. Jung states:

> "We must now turn to the question of how the existence of archetypes can be proved. Since archetypes are supposed to produce certain psychic forms, we must discuss how and where one can get hold of the material demonstrating these forms. The main source, then, is dreams, which have the advantage of being involuntary, spontaneous products of the unconscious psyche and are therefore pure products of nature not falsified by any conscious purpose. By questioning the individual one can ascertain which of the motifs appearing in the dream are known to him. From those which are unknown to him we must naturally exclude all motifs which might be known to him" (CW, vol. 9 I, par. 100)

In 1909, Jung and Freud journeyed together to lecture in the United States. Aboard ship the two talked daily and would daily analyze each other's dreams. One particular dream that Jung had, and the difference in how each one interpreted the dream, directly impacted their impending break. In this dream Jung was:

> "Descending through several levels of a house, each level representing an earlier period of history, until at last he was in a low cave cut into a rock, with thick dust on the floor and in the dust scattered bones and broken pottery and a couple of human skulls, all like remains of a primitive culture" (Singer 1972, p. 305).

For Freud, this dream represented a manifestation of a death wish directed towards him. For Jung however, the dream was highly significant in symbolic terms, representing "a ritual of passage from the personal conscious into the collective unconscious, where the remnants of his archaic heritage rested" (Singer 1972, p. 305).

In addition to believing that the symbols which occur in hallucinations and dreams are evidence of a collective unconscious and of archetypes, Jung also believed the symbols that are used in myths and fairy tales as similar evidence. Herein lies another overlap between the sociologies of Durkheim and

Jung. Durkheim was profoundly influenced by the early German psychologist, Wilhelm Wundt ([1887] 1916), who used myths and fairy tales in developing "folk psychology."

In the following section the collective unconscious and archetypes will be considered in more detail and in terms of their sociological implications.

THE SOCIOLOGY OF THE COLLECTIVE UNCONSCIOUS & ARCHETYPES

As previously stated, just as the collective consciousness is a representation for Durkheim, the collective unconscious is an archetype for Jung. Greenwood states: "A comparison of Durkheim's collective consciousness and Jung's collective unconscious reveals strikingly similar concepts" (Greenwood 1990, p. 1). It may not be by chance that there is also a striking similarity between Durkheim's collective representations and Jung's archetypes. As also noted earlier, both concepts were used by their mutual friend Levy-Bruhl. Jung states:

> "I have no system, no doctrine, nothing of that kind. I am an empiricist, with no metaphysical views at all. I have only hypotheses. From them I have gained some basic principles. There is the self, which is the totality of one's being, known and unknown, conscious and unconscious as opposed to the distinction between physical and psychic. Then there are the archetypes, those images of instinct. For instinct is not just an outward thrust, it also takes part in the representation of forms ... Instinct is not only biological, it is also ... from which can be studied down the ages among all people. These are archetypes ... There is also the collective unconscious, that immense treasury, that great reservoir, whence mankind draws the images, the forces, which it translates into very different languages." (in McGuire: pgs. 414-415)

Here Jung has described himself as an empiricist, not tied to any dogma. He identifies an unconscious collective aspect to human existence and he identifies archetypes. Archetypes are said to be related to the notion of instinct and are biologically based with a spiritual dimension. Images or archetypes emerge from the vast collective unconscious. The forms of these images can be studied because they repeat themselves over time. The sociological significance of the collective unconscious lies in its universal nature as revealed in the following distinction of the personal unconscious and the collective unconscious made by Jung:

> "[The] distinction between the personal unconscious and the collective unconscious ... is that the personal would be more involved with the immediate life of the individual, and the collective would be universal, having the same elements in all men [everyone]." (in McGuire and Hull 1977, p. 321)

The personal unconscious is attained by individual experiences and varies accordingly, but the collective unconscious is attained by everyone and is the same for everyone:

> "[There are] two layers in the unconscious... personal unconscious and an impersonal or transpersonal unconscious ... [or] collective unconscious- because it is detached from anything personal and is common to all men [everyone], since its contents can be found everywhere." (CW: vol. 7, p. 103)

Again, the collective unconscious is universal in its nature whereas the personal unconscious is individual specific.

> "the collective unconscious, unlike the personal unconscious, is one and the same everywhere, in all individuals, just as all biological functions and all instincts are the same in members of the same species." (CW: vol. 10. p. 450)

As members of a common species, human beings have collective biological functions and instincts; so too, do we all have a universal collective conscious. This position compliments Durkheim's notion of the collective consciousness which is culturally specific.

> "The collective unconscious is a part of the psyche which can be negatively distinguished from a personal unconscious by the fact that it does not, like the latter, owe its existence to personal experience and consequently is not a personal acquisition." (CW: vol. 9 I, p. 42)

The personal unconscious develops through personal experience; however the collective unconscious simple is.

> "The collective unconscious is ... identical in all men [all humans] and thus constitutes a common psychic substrate of a suprapersonal nature which is present in every one of us." (CW: vol. 9 I, p. 3)

From these quotes we can see that for Jung the collective unconscious is that aspect of the unconscious that is both impersonal and universal. Further, Jung believed that the collective unconscious consisted of modes of behavior that he refers to as "typical modes of apprehension" (CW: vol. 8, p. 137) which he calls archetypes.

> "The concept of the archetype, which is an indispensable correlate of the idea of the collective unconscious, indicates the existence of definite forms in the psyche which seem to be present always and everywhere." (CW: vol. 9 I, p. 42)

The concepts of archetypes and the collective unconscious are interdependent. Archetypes suggest a universal form that is universally present.

"[The] a priori existence of 'organizing factors,' the archetypes, which are to be understood as inborn modes of functioning that constitute, in their totality, man's [human] nature. The chick does not learn how to come out of the egg – it possesses this knowledge a priori." (CW: vol. 5, p. 328)

Jung is saying that the notion of <u>tabula rasa</u> is incorrect in terms of the human experience (except maybe for the personal unconscious). Human beings are viewed as having unlearned, inborn tendencies.

"[Archetypes are] ... not ... racial heredity, but of a universally human characteristic. Nor is it a question of inherited ideas, but of a functional disposition to produce the same, or very similar ideas ..." (CW: vol. 5, p. 102)

Here Jung is addressing the issue of form vs. content or substance. It is not the idea, substance, or content of the archetype that is inherited. It is the disposition to use archetypal forms that is inherited. The content is shaped by the given culture and its collective history.

"The human mind possesses general and typical modes of functioning which correspond to the biological 'patter of behavior'. These preexistent, innate patterns – the archetypes – can easily produce in the most widely differing individuals' ideas or combinations of ideas that are practically identical, and whose origin no individual experience can be made responsible..." (CW: vol. 5, p. 313)

Archetypes as a biological cause for human ideas are pointed to. Archetypes or their inherent forms are consistent throughout our species; the explanation for which cannot be reduced to the individual level.

"[Archetypes are] ... not a question of inherited ideas, but of an inborn disposition to produce parallel thought-formations, or rather of identical psychic structures common to all men [everyone], which I... called the archetypes of the unconscious. They correspond to the concept of the 'pattern of behavior' in biology..." (CW: vol. 5, p. 158)

In the following quote, Jung again emphasizes the continuous and collective input into the collective unconsciousness by all of our species that have lived before us (prehistoric and historic).

"The archetypal contents of the (collected) unconscious, [is] the archaic heritage of humanity, the legacy left behind by all differentiation and... development... [that is] bestowed upon all men [everyone] like sunshine and air." (CW: vol. 5, p. 178)

CHAPTER VI

CONCLUSION

It is with some irony that I advocate listening to the faint voices from the past of two "dead European guys" as a means for both understanding human existence in the present and for anticipating our collective future. The voices of Emile Durkheim and Carl Jung are but slight whispers and difficult to hear as one reads their writings. However if one reads, contemplates, and reflects on their writings, then Durkheim's and Jung's voices grow louder and clearer. Instead of Durkheim and Jung becoming less relevant, over time, in understanding societal and individual existence, they have actually become more relevant. A "cross-fertilization" of ideas between Europe and the United States has taken place as the result of the works of Durkheim and Jung.

Over the present century, the increasing fragmentation, splintering and isolation of academic disciplines seems a proper metaphor for the individual's experience. The interdisciplinary approaches of Durkheim and Jung offer the potential to help heal academia's schizoid affliction. Durkheim was much more than just a sociologist, as Jung was much more than just a psychologist. For example, the sociology of Durkheim is never without concern for the individual citizen. The psychology of Jung is never without concern for the collectivity. Anthropology is but one of the other disciplines that can benefit from Durkheim's and Jung's interdisciplinary approach.

Although 20th century psychology has made the individual psyche the focal point and 20th century sociology emphasizes the collectivity, I suggest that there is not one single means of achieving what I have termed "wholeness." Wholeness is possible through individual consciousness, collective consciousness, the individual unconscious, and the collective unconscious or any combination of these for aspects. Wholeness is defined here as the integration of these four aspects. Suggesting the interpretation of these four aspects as the foundation for wholeness implies that non-integration of these aspects results in non-wholeness. There seems to be some parallel between this idea and the biological model of DNA. The DNA code, although consisting of only four different elements in altering combinations, is responsible for the incredible variety we find in and between each and every human being. With my proposed model, I am suggesting, in part, that as social or human being, each of us consists, in varying combinations, of the named aspects.

In considering individual consciousness, I have argued that the very notion "individual" only arises or develops within the collectivity and that likewise; "consciousness" arises from unconsciousness.

There can not be such a thing as an "individual" without a social context. Too, consciousness may exist only within the context of the unconscious. One implication of this position is that we live in an irrational world, believing it to be rational. In part, chaos theory suggests that, rather than chaos being an aspect or interruption of our stable physical world, the reality is that our stable physical world is an aspect or interruption within a context of chaos.

Wholeness, as a concept, is both a collective representation and an archetype. Wholeness is archetypal because its basic form is found universally throughout societies past and present. Wholeness as a collective representation varies across societies because collective representations are cultural specific. For example, the notions of collective representation and archetype applied to the concept "wholeness" can and do yield very different results.

Kahlil Gibran once said: "The light of stars that were extinguished ages ago still reaches us. So it is with great men who died centuries ago, but still reach us with the radiations of their personality." This may be even more true of those that have been deceased for only decades, as with social theorists such as Durkheim, Freud, and Jung. As we move out of the 20th century and closer to the 21st, it is with some irony that there is so much yet to be gleaned from dead thinkers. They lie dead, but their thoughts live and are yet to bear full fruit.

Durkheim's call for a sociology that incorporates the concepts of the unconscious and collective representations is being echoed by Mestrovic. If a "reformation of sociology" is to take place, the cultural and universal aspects of Jung's thoughts are pertinent, for much of Jung's work parallels Durkheim's thoughts. The collective unconscious and archetypes may have the potential for explaining cultural universals such as family, religion and the nation. These same notions can also lead to better understandings on cultural levels, on the level of individuals, and on the personal level.

REFERENCES

Alpert, Harry. 1939. <u>Emile Durkheim and His Sociology.</u>
New York: Columbia University Press.

_____. 1939b. "Emile Durkheim and Sociologismic Psychology."
<u>American Journal of Sociology,</u> 45: 64-70.

_____. 1958. "Emile Durkheim: Enemy of Fixed Psychological Elements."
<u>American Journal of Sociology,</u> 62: 662-4.

Bellah, Robert N., Richard Madsen, William M. Sullivan, Ann Swidler, and
Steven M. Tipton. 1985. <u>Habits of the Heart.</u>
New York: Perennial Library.

Bennet, E. A. 1967. <u>What Jung Really Said</u>. New York: Schocken Books.

Cladis, Mark S. 1992. <u>A Communitarian Defense of Liberalism: Emile Durkheim and
Contemporary Social Theory</u>. Stanford: Stanford University Press.

Cook, A. Gary. 1993. <u>George Herbert Mead: The Making of a social Pragmatist.</u>
Chicago: University of Illinois Press.

Crescimanno, Russell. 1982. <u>Culture, Consciousness, and Beyond: An Introduction</u>.
New York: University Press of America.

Durkheim, Emile. (1893) 1965. <u>The Division of Labor in Society,</u>
Translated by George Simpson. New York: The Free Press.

_____. (1898a) 1973. "Individual and Collective Representations." Pp. 1-34 in
<u>Sociology and Philosophy</u> by E. Durkheim. New York: The Free Press.

_____. (1898b) 1973. "Individualism and the Intellectuals." Pp. 43-60 in <u>Emile</u>

Durkheim on Morality and Society, by Robert Bellah (ed). Chicago: The University of Chicago Press.

_____. (1914) 1973. "The Dualism of Human Nature and Its Social Conditions." Pp. 149-66 in Emile Durkheim on Morality and Society, edited by R. Bellah. Chicago: University of Chicago Press.

_____. (1915) 1965. The Elementary Forms of the Religious Life, translated by Joseph Ward Swain. New York: Free Press.

_____. (1897) 1966. Suicide. New York: The Free Press.

_____. (1924) 1974. Sociology and Philosophy, translated by D. F. Pocock. New York: Free Press.

_____. (1925) 1963. Moral Education, translated by E. K. Wilson and Herman Schnurer. Glencoe, Ill.; Free Press.

_____. (1950) 1983. Professional Ethics and Civil Morals, translated by C. Brookfield. Westport, Conn: Greenwood Press, Publishers.

_____. (1990). Emile Durkheim: Critical Assessments. New York: Routledge.

Durkheim, Emil and Marcel Mauss. 1975. Primitive Classification. Chicago: The University of Chicago Press.

Ellenberger, Henri F. 1970. The Discovery of the Unconscious. New York: Basic Books.

Fauconnet, Paul. (1933) 1958. "Introduction to the Original Education." Pp. 27-57 in Education and Sociology, by E. Durkheim. Glencoe, Ill: Free Press.

Featherstone, M. 1988. "In Pursuit of the Postmodern: An Introduction." Theory, Culture and Society, 5(2-3): 195-216.

Freud, Sigmund. (1923) 1974. "The Id and the Ego." Pp.1-59 of The Standard Edition of
        the Complete Psychological Works of Sigmund Freud, editorship of James Strachey, Volume
        XIX. London: Hogarth.

_____. 1938. The Basic Writings of Sigmund Freud, edited by A. Brill. New York:
        Random House.

_____. 1964. The Standard Edition of the Complete Psychological Works of Sigmund
        Freud, editorship of James Strachey, volume XVIII. London: Hogarth Press.

Goldbrunner, Josef. 1966. Individuation. Notre Dame: Notre Dame Press.

Greenwood, Susan F. 1990. "Emile Durkheim and C. G. Jung: Structuring A
        Transpersonal Sociology and Religion." Journal for the Scientific Study of Religion. Dec.
Halbwachs, Maurice. 1980. The Collective Memory. New York: Harper & Row,
        Publishers.

Harman, Willis W. 1988. Global Mind Change: the Promise of the Last Years of the
        Twentieth Century. Indianapolis, Ind: Knowledge Systems.

Hillman, James. 1975. Revising Psychology. New York: Harper and Row, Publishers.

Hopcke, Robert H. 1989. A Guided Tour of the Collected Works of C. G. Jung. Boston:
        Shambhala.

Jaffe, Aniela. 1970. The Myth of Meaning in the Work of C. G. Jung. Zurich: Daimon.

Jacobi, Jolande. 1959. Complex/Archetype/Symbol in the Psychology of C. G. Jung.
        Princeton: Princeton Press.

_____. 1973. The Psychology of C. G. Jung. New Haven: Yale University Press.

Jung, Carl G. 1960. <u>Collected Works of Carl G. Jung, vol. 3</u>. Princeton: Princeton Press.

_____. 1960. <u>Collected Works of Carl G. Jung, vol. 8.</u> Princeton: Princeton Press.

_____. 1961. <u>Collected Works of Carl G. Jung, vol. 4.</u> Princeton: Princeton Press.

_____. 1967. <u>Collected Works of Carl G. Jung, vol. 5.</u> Princeton: Princeton Press.

_____. 1966. <u>Collected Works of Carl G. Jung, vol. 7.</u> Princeton: Princeton Press.

_____. 1969. <u>Collected Works of Carl G. Jung, vol. 9.</u> Princeton: Princeton Press.

_____. 1964. <u>Collected Works of Carl G. Jung, vol. 10.</u> Princeton: Princeton Press.

_____. 1966. <u>Collected Works of Carl G. Jung, vol. 15.</u> Princeton: Princeton Press.

LaCapra, Dominick. 1972. <u>Emile Durkheim: Sociologist and Philosopher</u>. Ithaca: Cornell University Press.

Levin, Malinda Jo. 1978. <u>Psychology: A Biographical Approach</u>. New York: McGraw-Hill Company.

Logan, Richard D. 1987. "Historical Change in Prevailing Sense of Self." in <u>Self & Identity: Psychosocial Perspectives</u>. New York: John Wiley & Sons.

Luckman, Thomas. 1967. <u>The Invisible Religion</u>. New York: Macmillan Company.

Lukes, Steven. 1967. "Prolegomena to the Interpretation of Durkheim." in <u>European Journal of Sociology</u>, 12: 183-209.

_____. 1972. <u>Emile Durkheim: His Life and Work</u>. New York: Harper &Row.

Magee, B. 1983. The Philosophy of Schopenhauer. New York: Oxford University Press.

Markley, O. W. and Willis Harman. 1982. Changing Images of Man. New York:
    Pergamon Press.

Matoon, Mary Ann. 1981. Jungian Psychology in Perspective. New York: Free Press.

McLuhan, Marshall. 1989. The Global Village: Transformation in World Life & Media
    in the 21st Century. New York: Oxford University Press.

Mead, George H. 1934. Mind, Self, and Society. Chicago: University of Chicago Press.

McGuire, William and R. F. C. Hull, (ed). 1977. C. G. Jung Speaking: Interviews &
    Encounters. Princeton: Princeton Press.

Mestrovic, Stjephan G. 1984. "Durkheim's Concept of the Unconscious." Current
    Perspectives in Social Theory. 5: 267-288. Greenwich, Conn: JAI Press.

_____. 1985. "Durkheim's Renovated Rationalism and the Idea that 'Collective Life is
    Only Made of Representations'." Current Perspectives in Social Theory. 6: 199-218. Greenwich,
    Conn: JAI Press.

_____. 1988. Emile Durkheim and the Reformation of Sociology. Totawa, NJ: Rowman
    & Littlefield.

_____. 1990. The Coming Fin De Siecle. New York: Routledge.

_____. 1991. "Mead and Durkheim on the Relationship of Fiction, Symbols, and
    Representation to Morality." Journal of Mental Imagery. (1/2): 141-46.

_____. 1992. Durkheim and Postmodern Culture. New York: Aldine deGruyter.

Newcomb, David R. 1993. "A Divergent Path: Emile Durkheim and Carl Jung." A paper presented at the 71st Meeting of the Southwester Social Science Association, Social Psychology Section, in New Orleans, March.

Parker, Ira. 1989. The Crisis in Modern Social Psychology and How to End It. New York: Routledge.

Progoff, Ira. 1953. Jung's Psychology and its Social Meaning. New York: Dialogue House Library.

Rosenfield, Israel. 1970. Freud: Character and Consciousness. New York: University Books.

Sherif, Muzafer and Hadley Cantril. (1947) 1966. The Psychology of Ego-Involvements. New York: John Wiley & Sons, Inc.

Singer, Junge. 1972. Boundaries of the Soul: the Practice of Jung's Psychology. New York: Doubleday.

Staude, John R. 1976. "From Depth Psychology to Depth Sociology: Freud, Jung, and Levi-Strauss." Theory and Society, fall 3(3), Pp. 303-338.

Stevens, Anthony. 1982. Archetypes: A Natural History of the Self. New York: Quill

Storr, Anthony. 1973. C. G. Jung. New York: Viking Press.

_____. 1983. The Essential Jung. Princeton: Princeton Press.

Wilber, Ken. 1981. Up From Eden: A Transpersonal View of Human Evolution. Garden City, NY: Anchor Books.

_____. 1983. Eye to Eye: The Quest for the New Paradigm. Garden City, NY: Anchor Books.

_____. 1984. <u>A Social God</u>. Boulder: New Science Library.

Willer, Judith. 1968. "The Implications of Durkheim's Philosophy of Science." <u>Kansas Journal of Sociology</u> 4(4): 175-90.

Wilmer, Harry A. 1987. <u>Practical Jung: Nuts and Bolts of Jungian Psychotherapy</u>. Wilmette, Ill.: Chiron Publications.

Winson, Jonathan. 1986. <u>Brain & Psyche: The Biology of the Unconscious</u>. New York: Vintage Book.

Wrong, Dennis. 1961. "The Over-Socialized Conception of Man in Modern Sociology." <u>American Sociological Review</u> 26:183-93.

Wundt, Wilhelm. (1887) 1916. <u>Elements of Folk Psychology: Outlines of Psychological History of the Development of Mankind</u>. London: Allen & Unwin.

Made in the USA
Las Vegas, NV
08 November 2023